Color your way to relaxation.

The health benefits of creativity are scientifically proven.
Making art is good for you!

....

In this always–connected, always on–demand life,
it's easy to spend the entire day consuming and responding
to all of the 'happenings' that absorb your time.
The simple act of coloring offers you some release from it all.

....

Take time out to color these beautiful images and you will be amazed at
the level of relaxation and calm you will achieve.
Your health and happiness will improve and you will be better for it.

....

The inspiration for this coloring book is Czech painter Alphonse Maria
Mucha who leapt to fame in Paris in 1895 when his poster Gismonda
(1894), created for the superstar Sarah Bernhardt, heralded the birth of
the distinctive 'Style Mucha' and established him as the pre-eminent
exponent of French Art Nouveau.

....

Two blank pages have been placed between each set of images to ensure
there is no bleed-through if using marker pens. Enjoy!

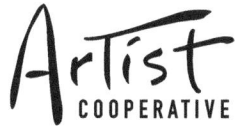

Artist
COOPERATIVE

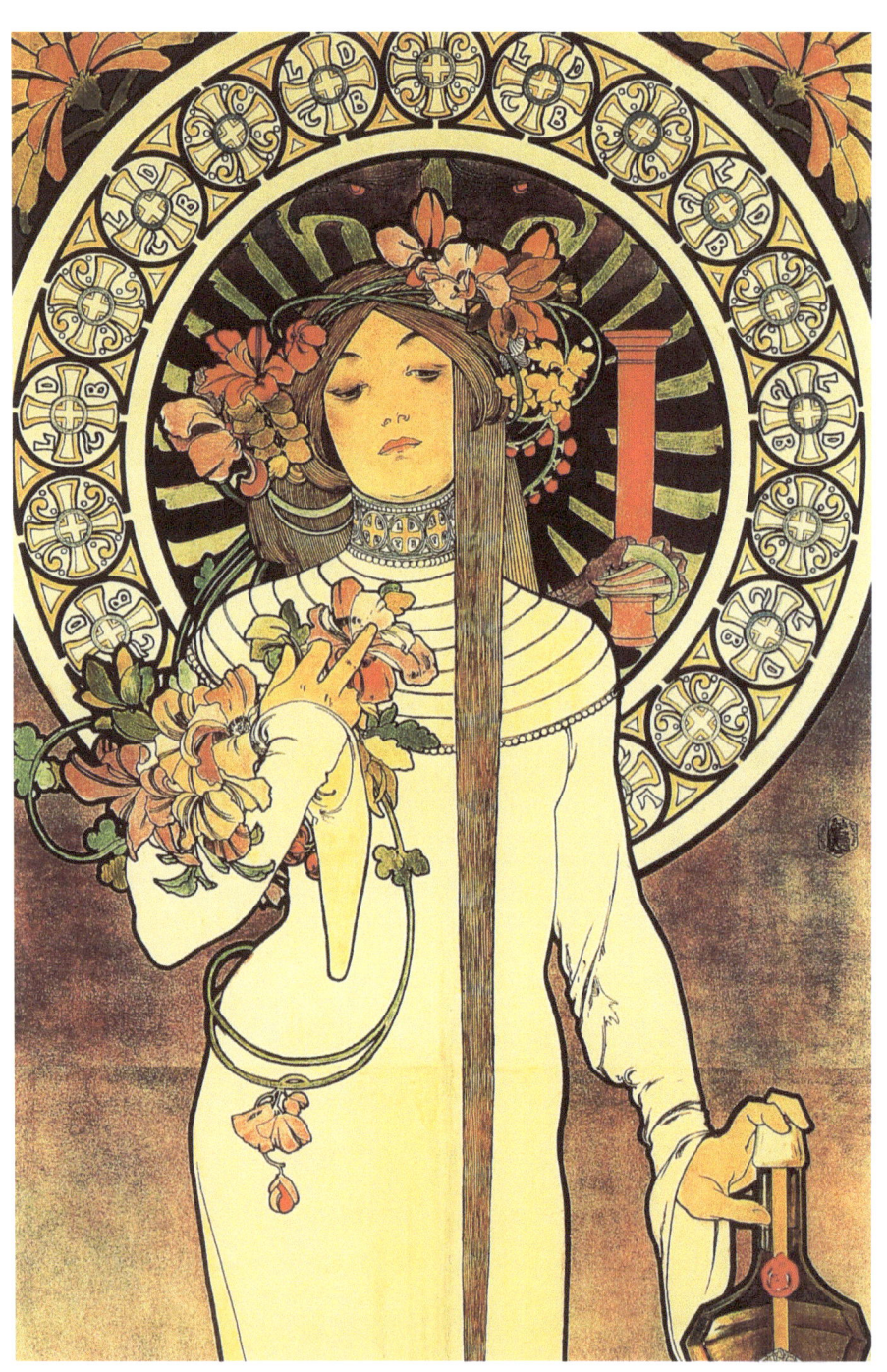

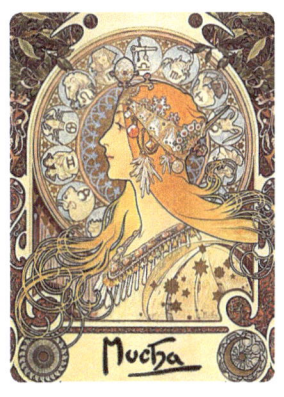
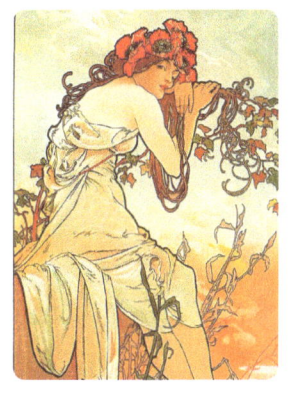
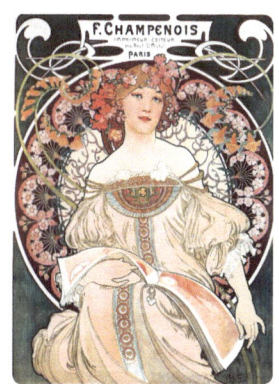
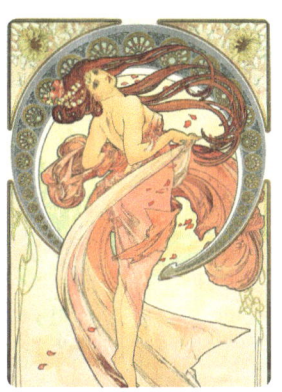
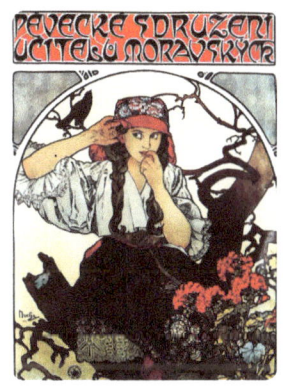
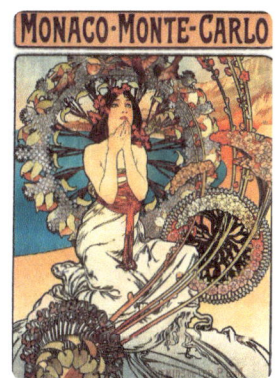
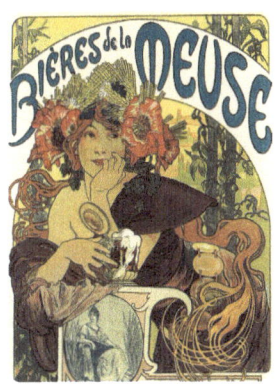
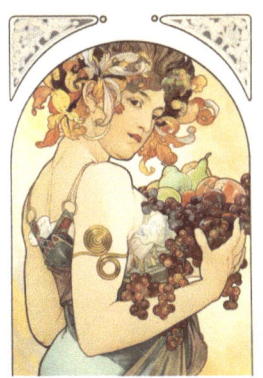
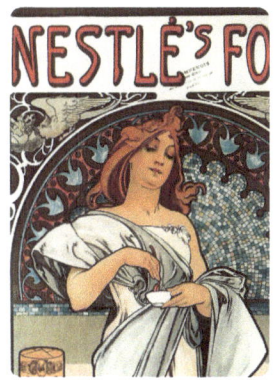

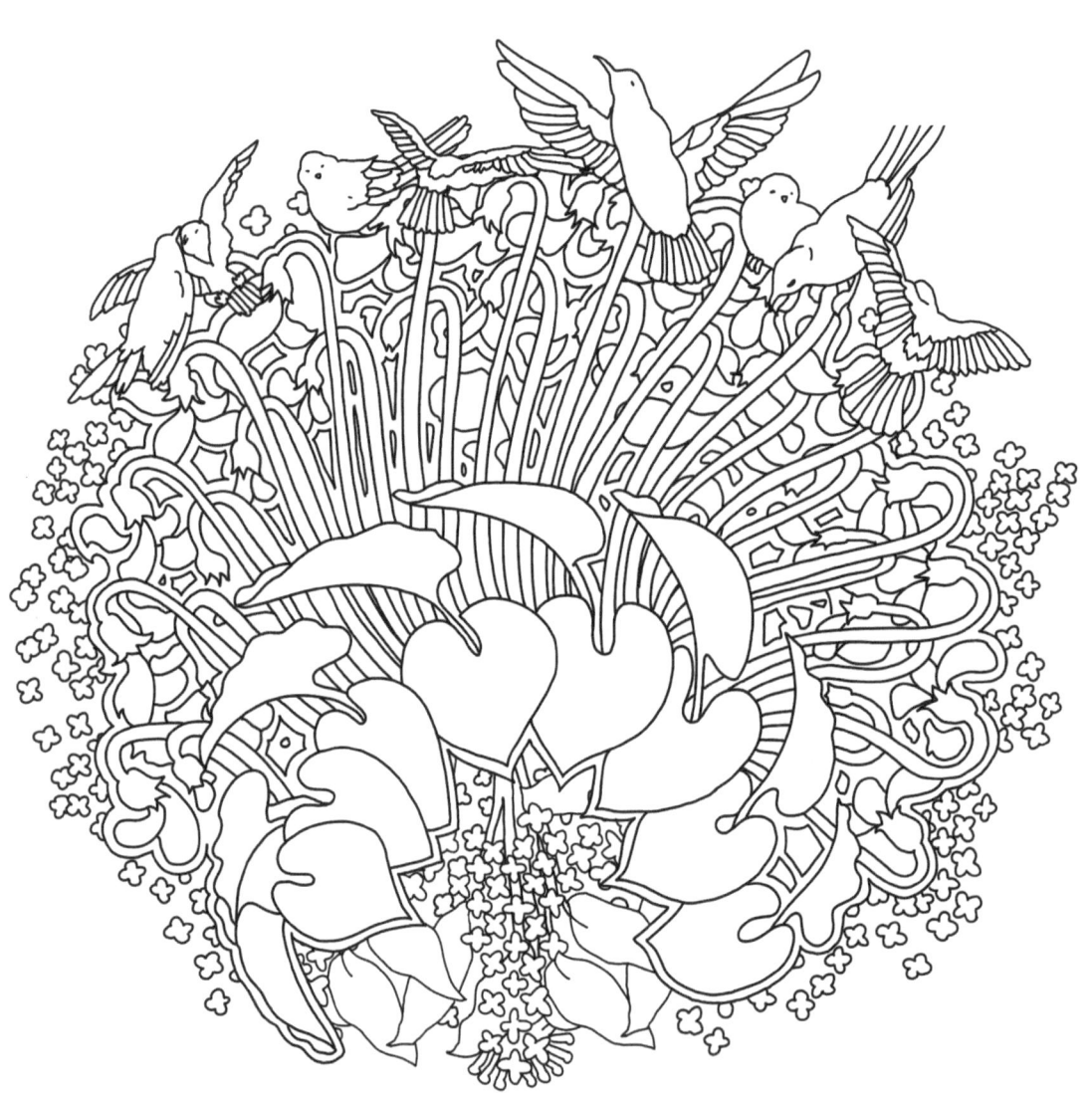

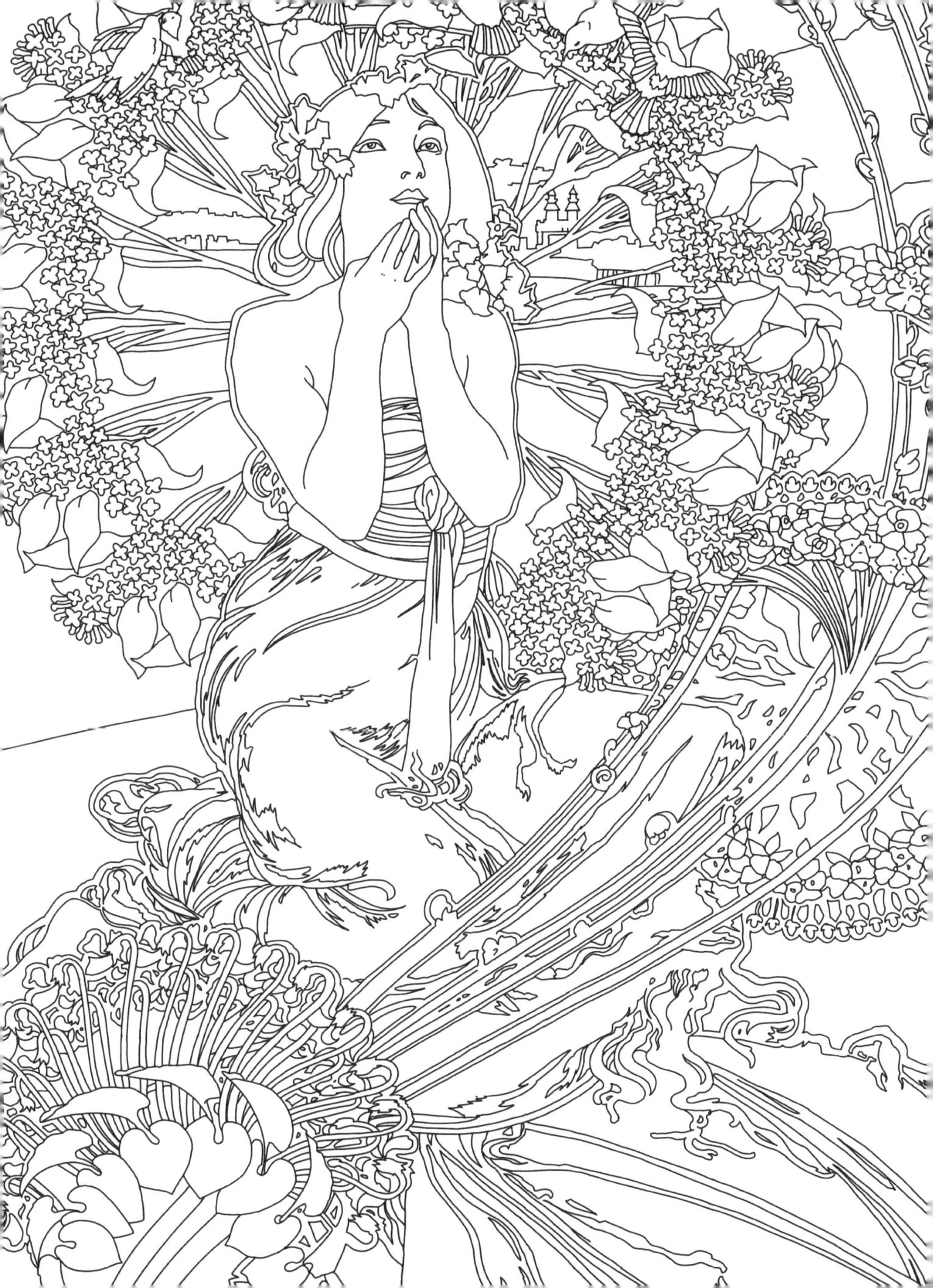

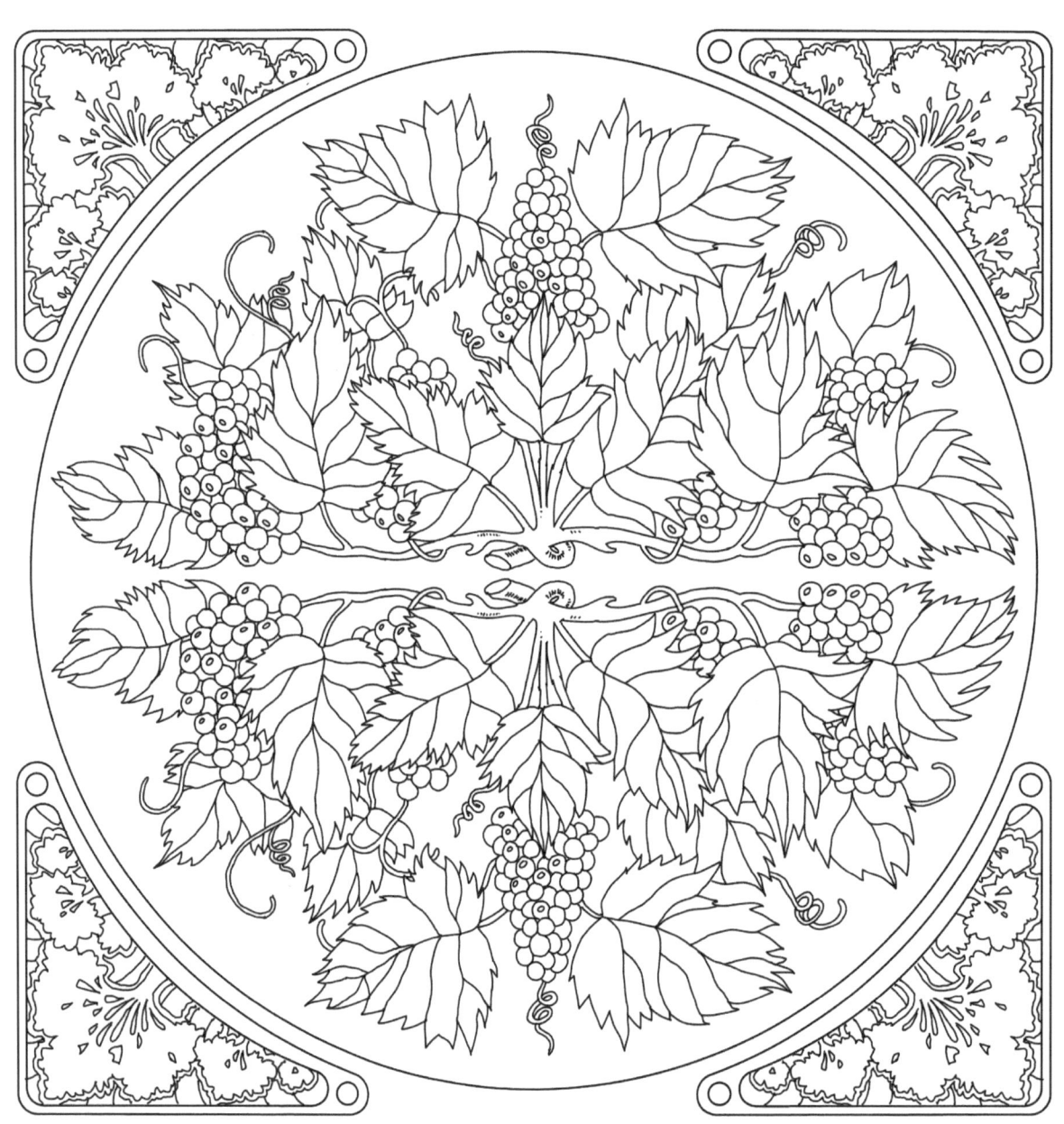

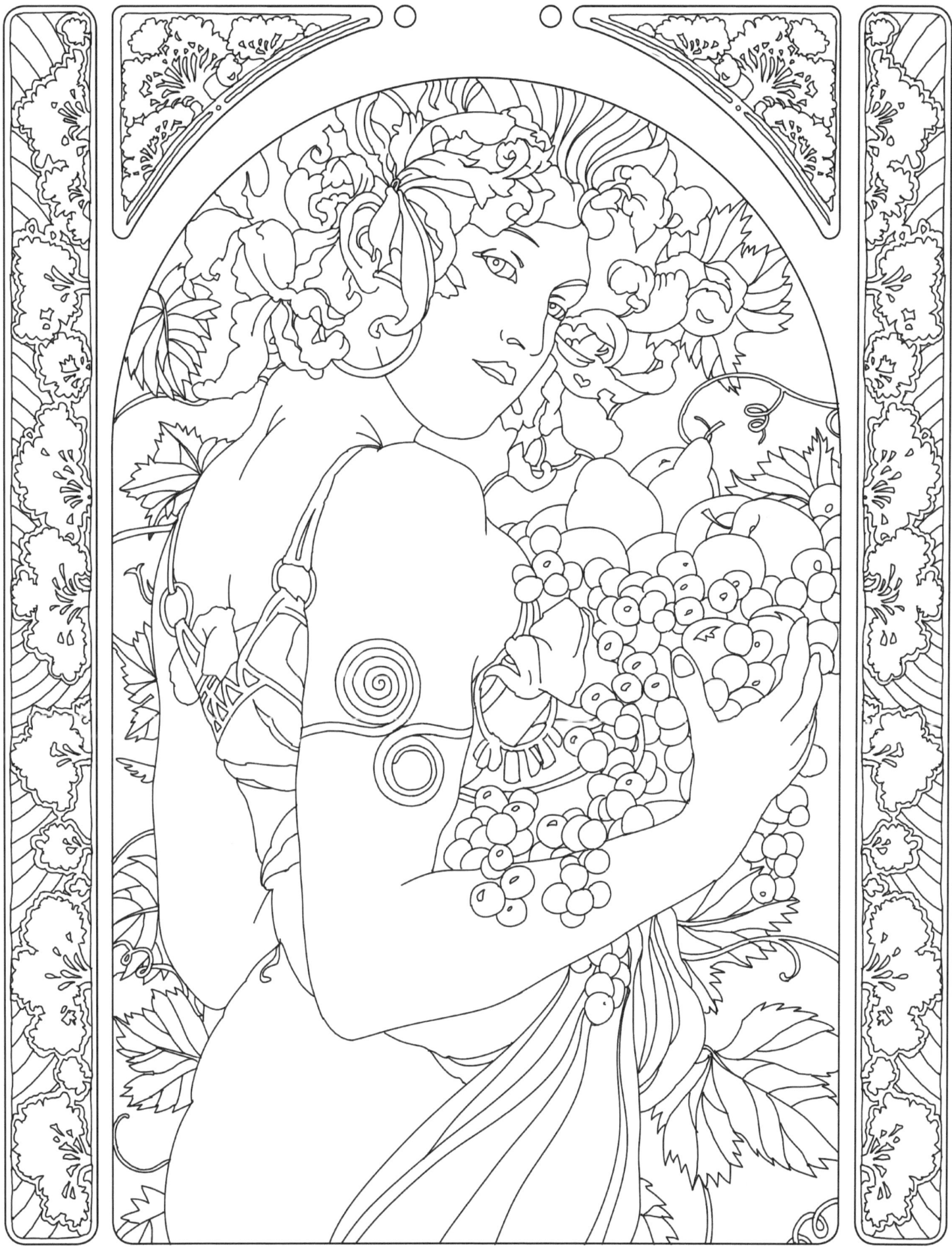

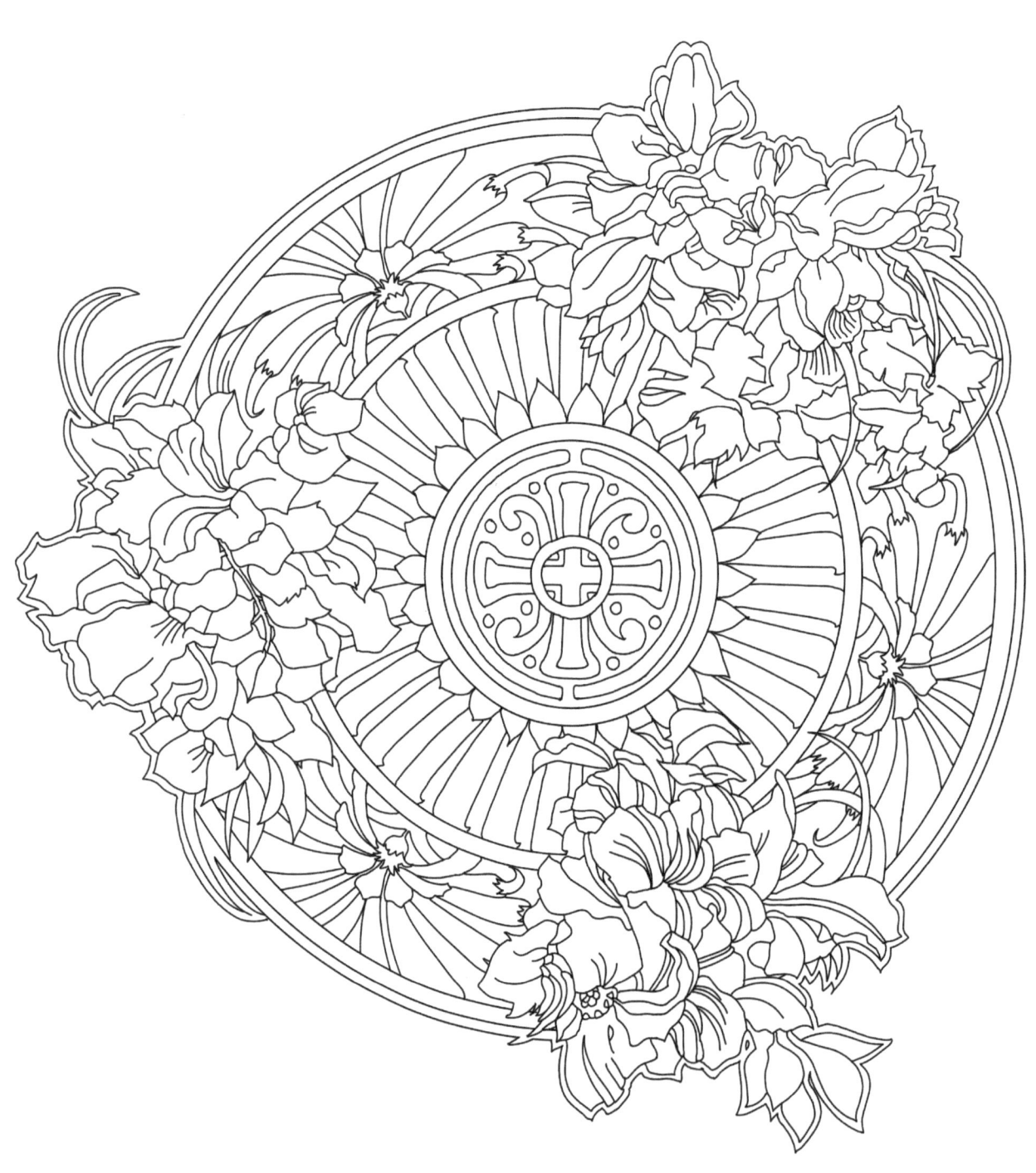

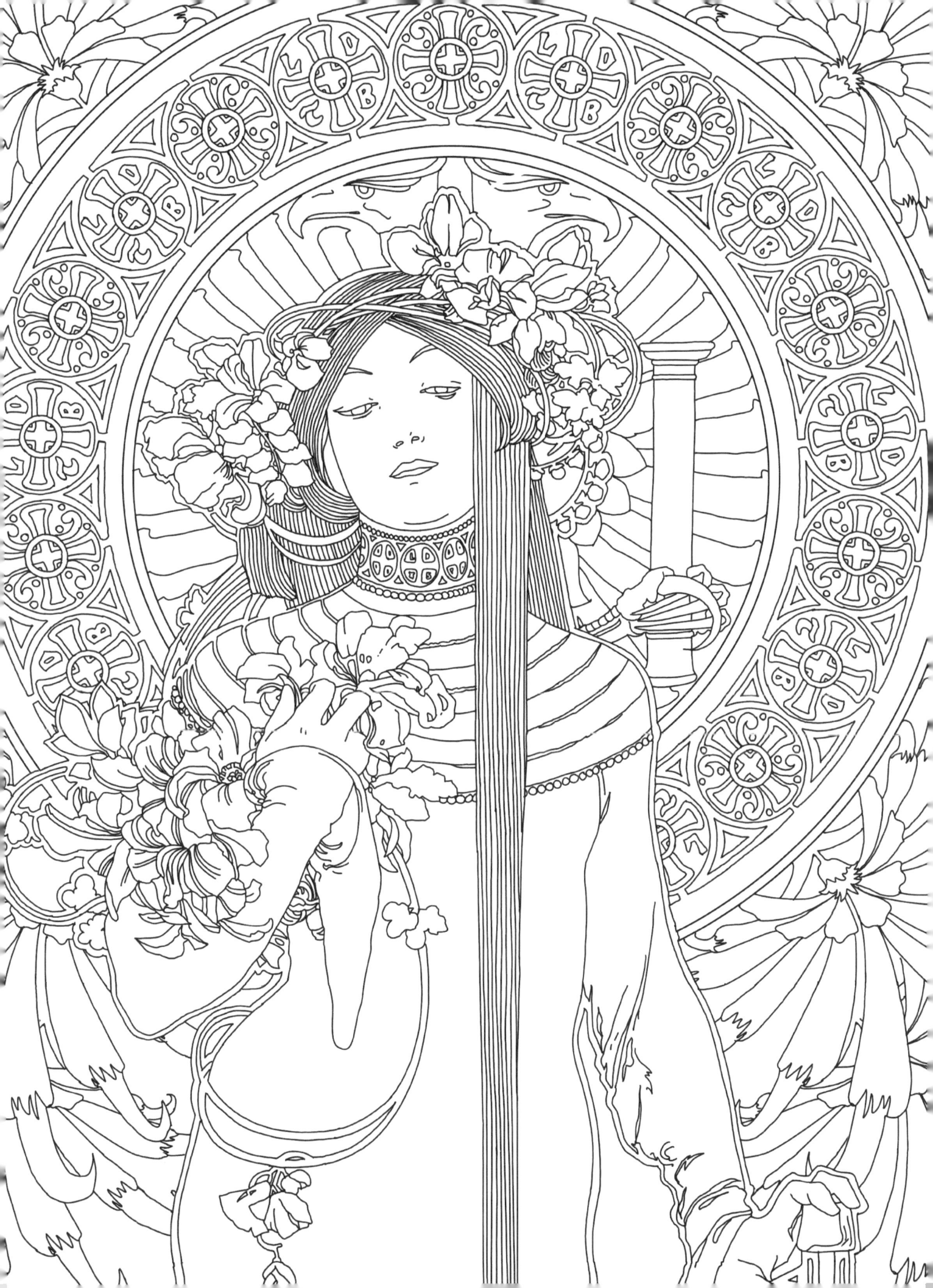

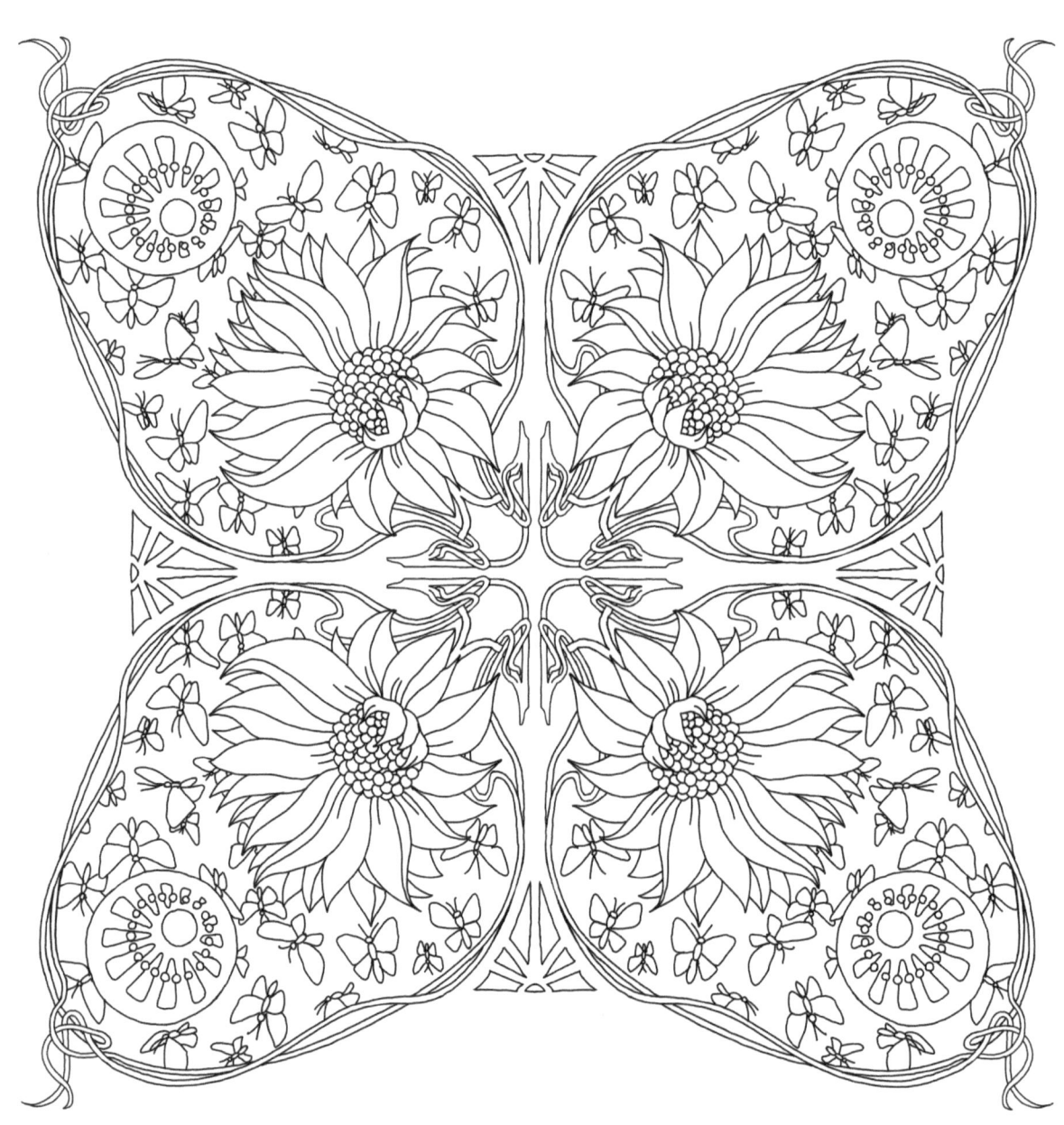

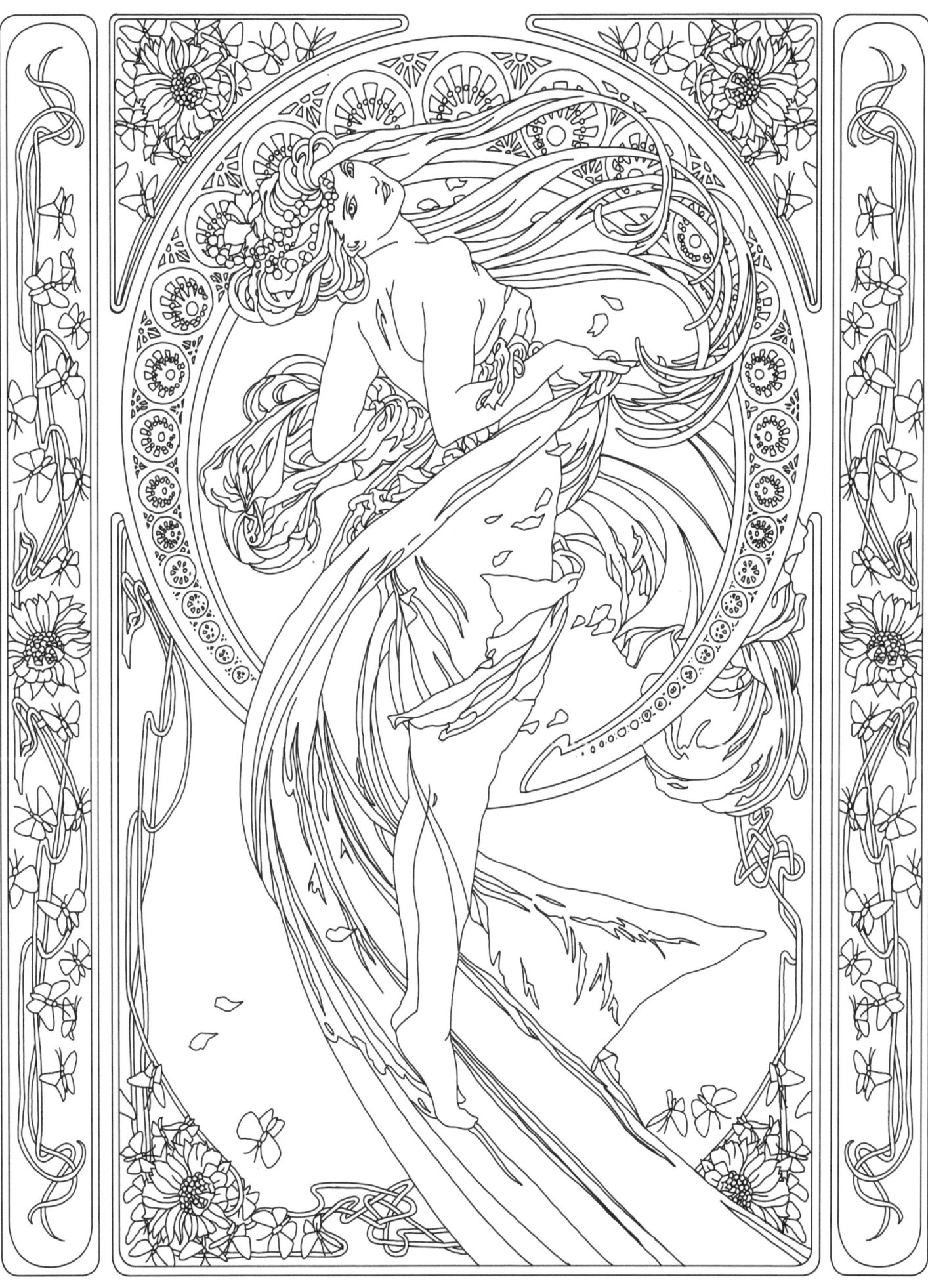

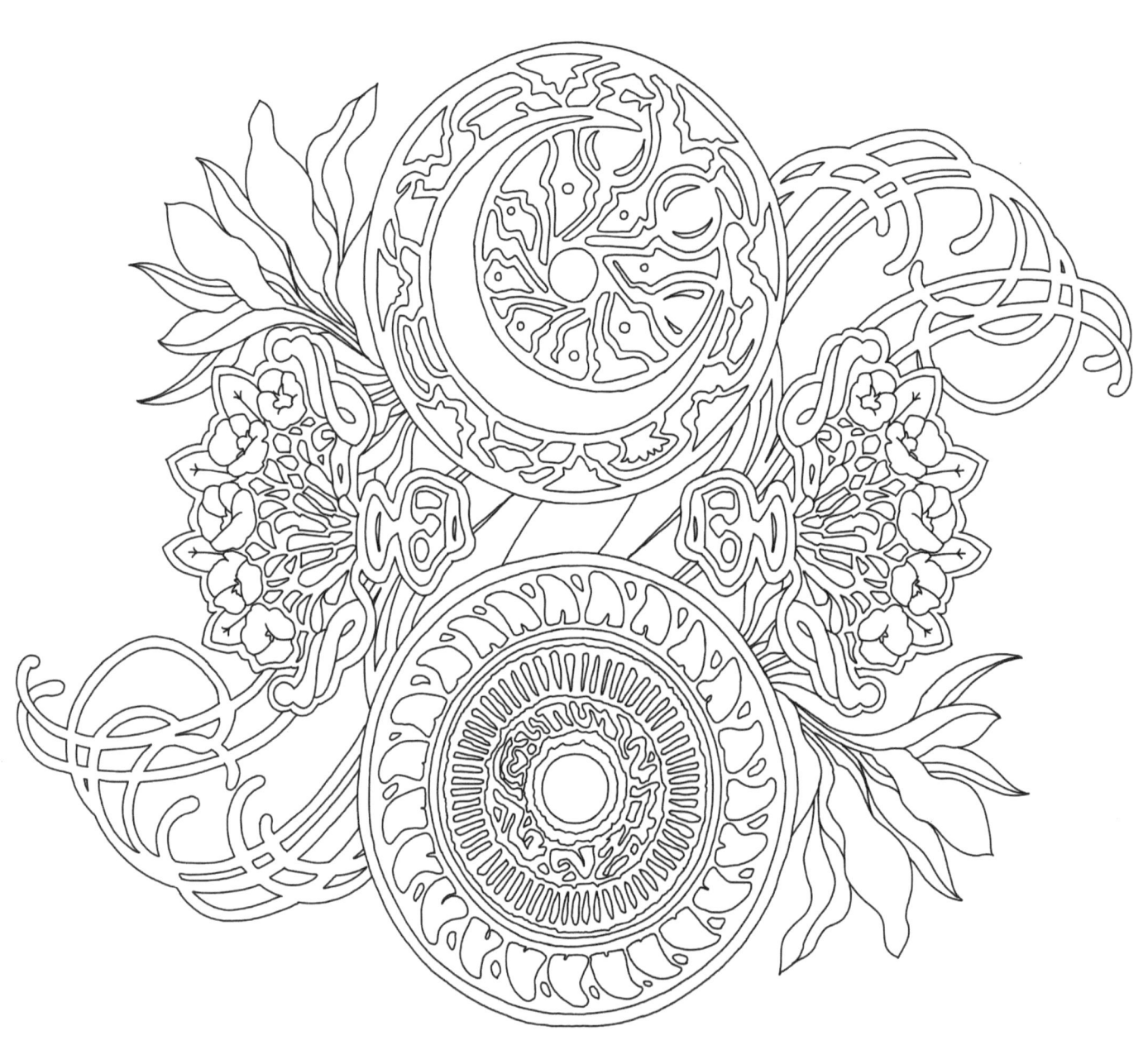

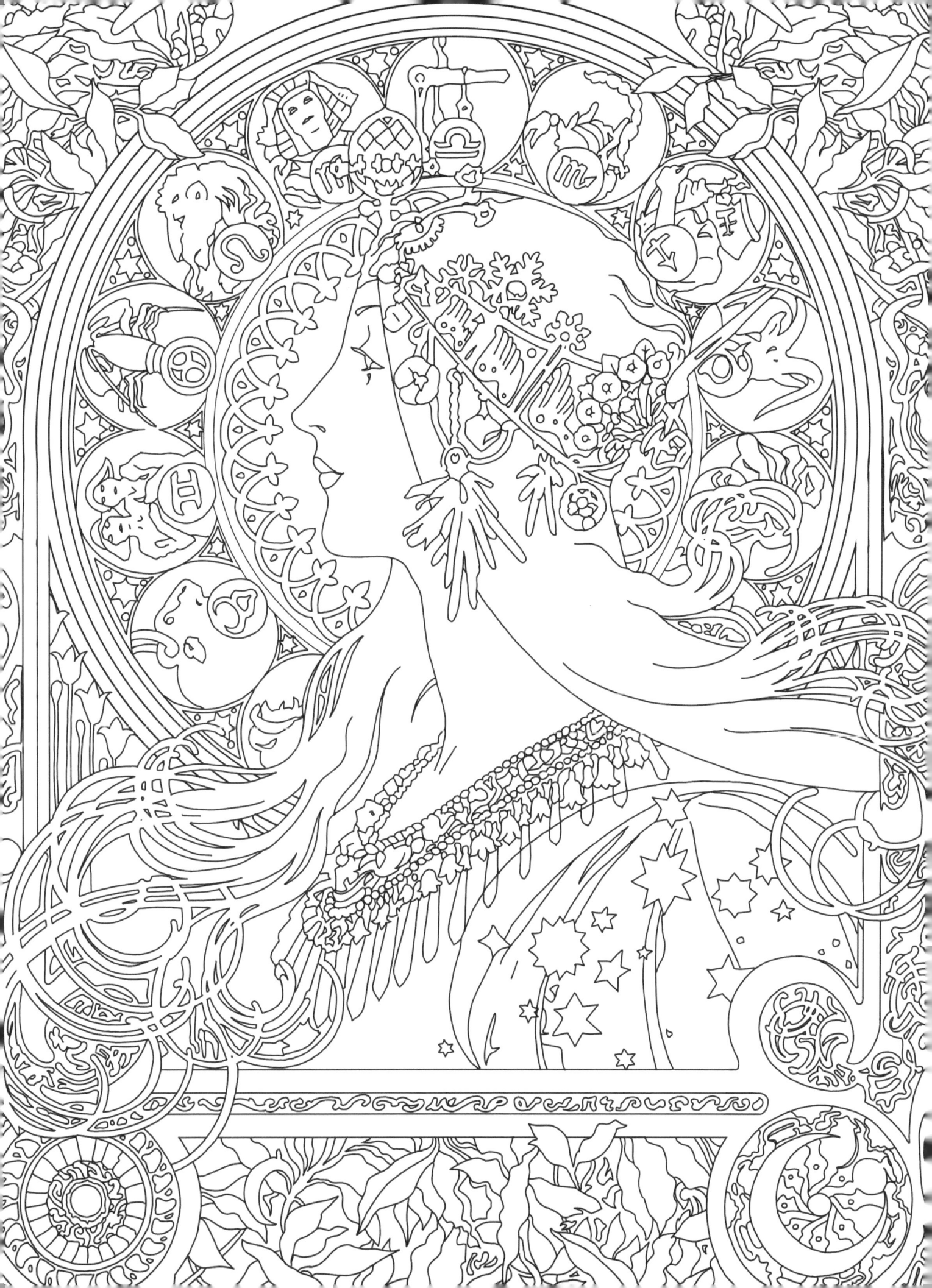

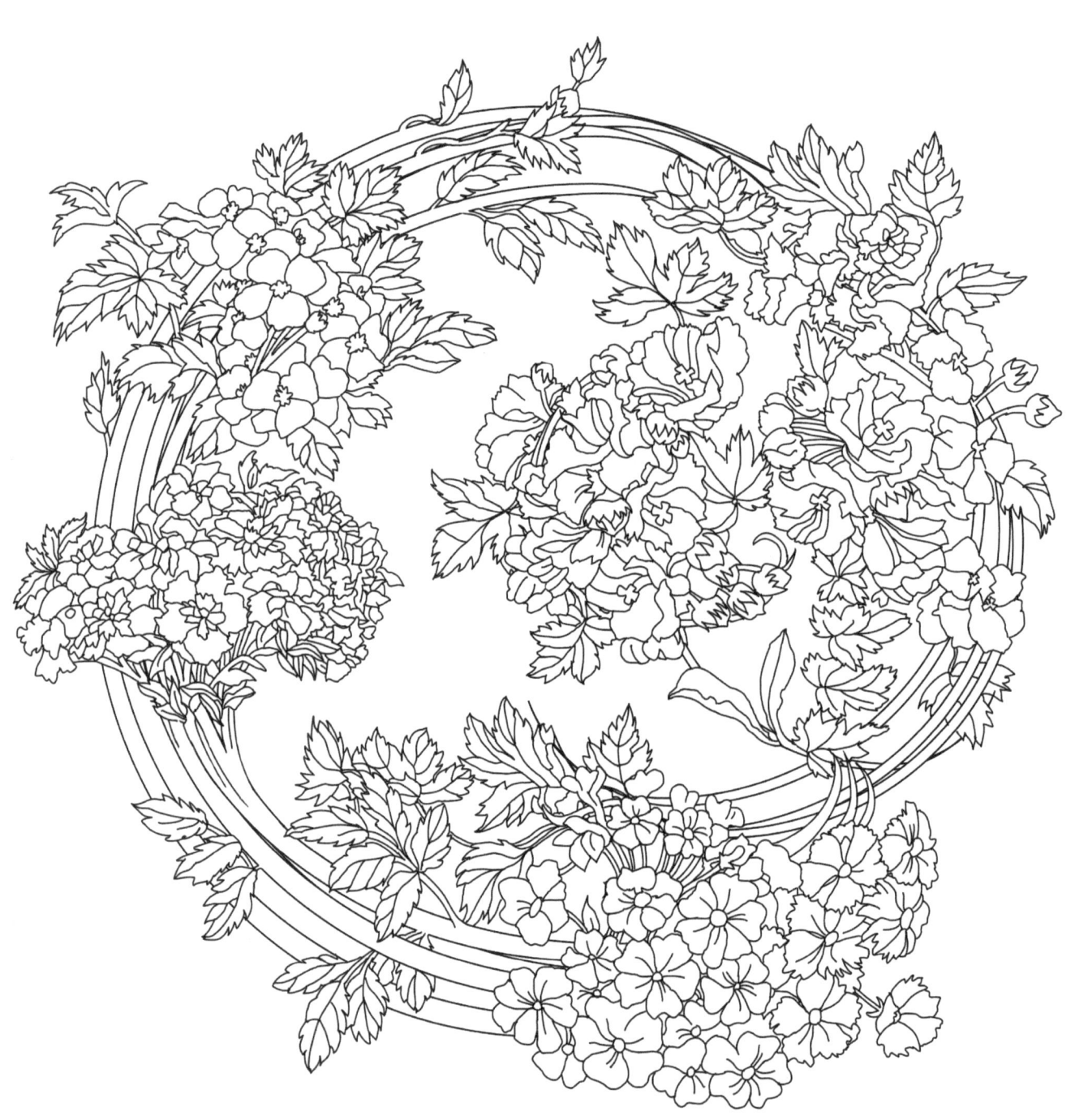

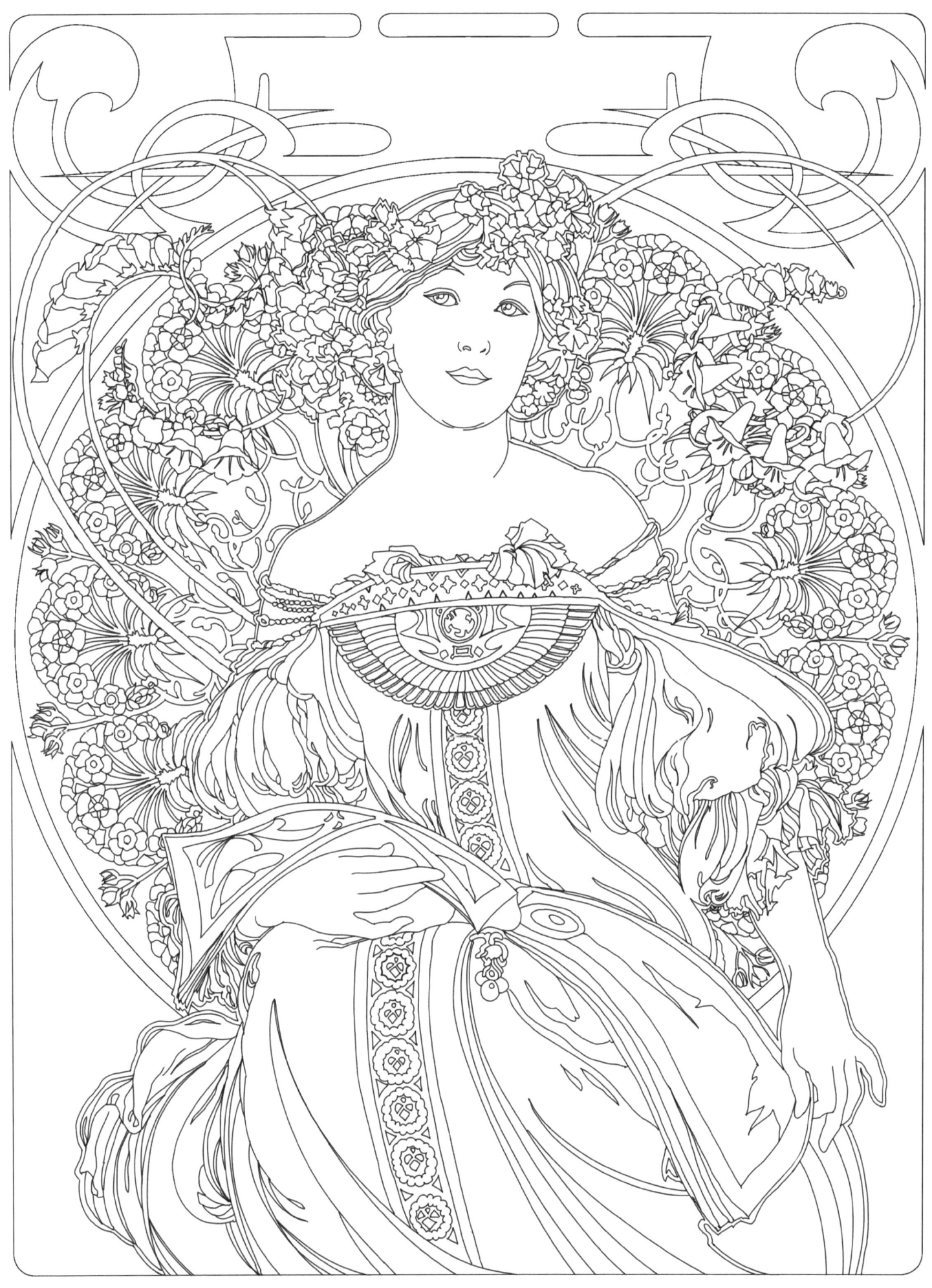

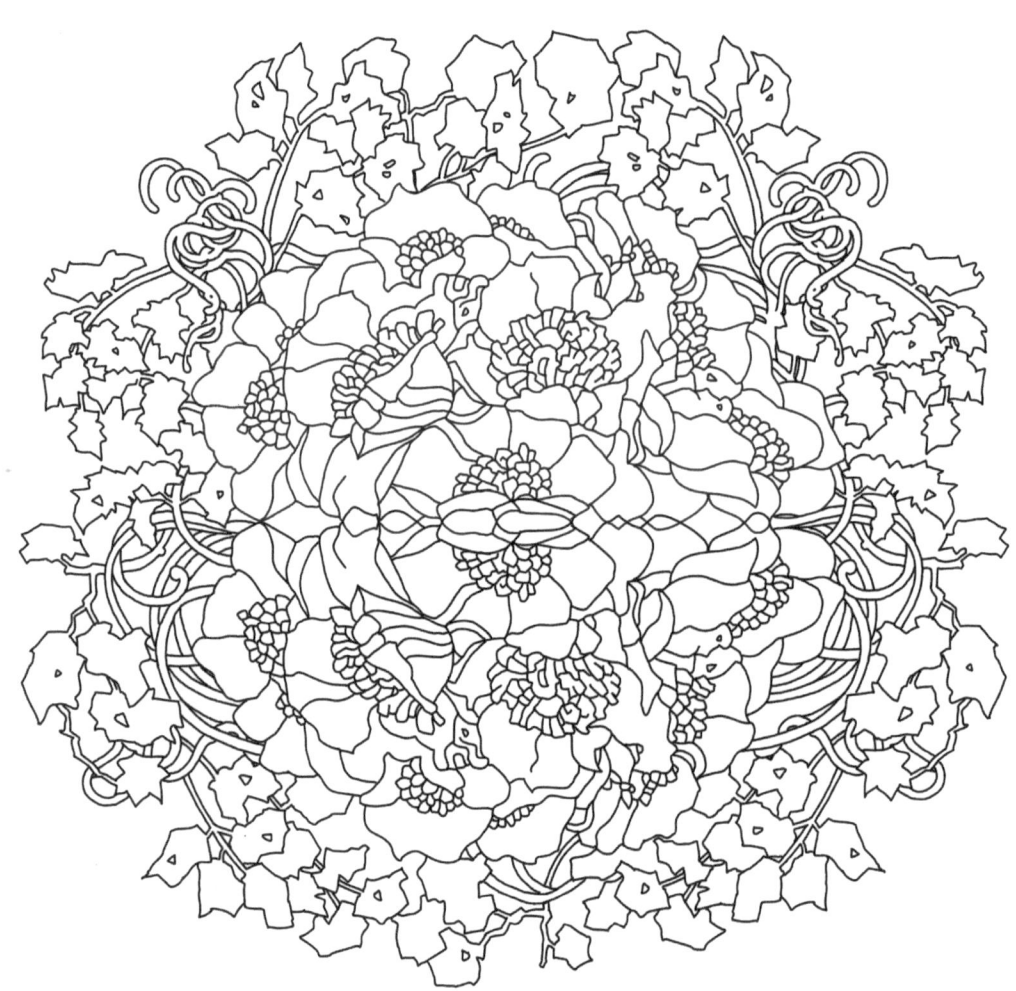

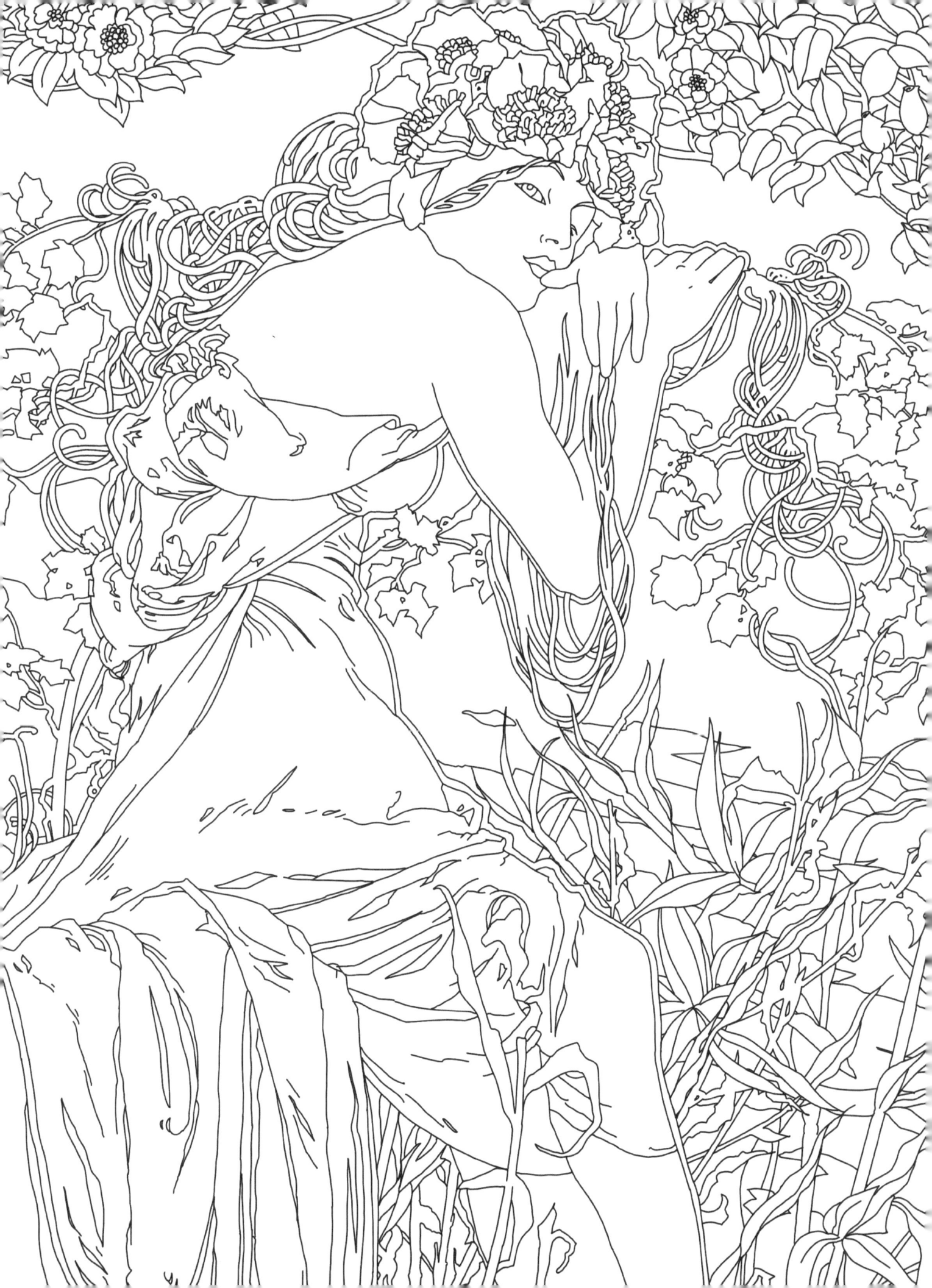

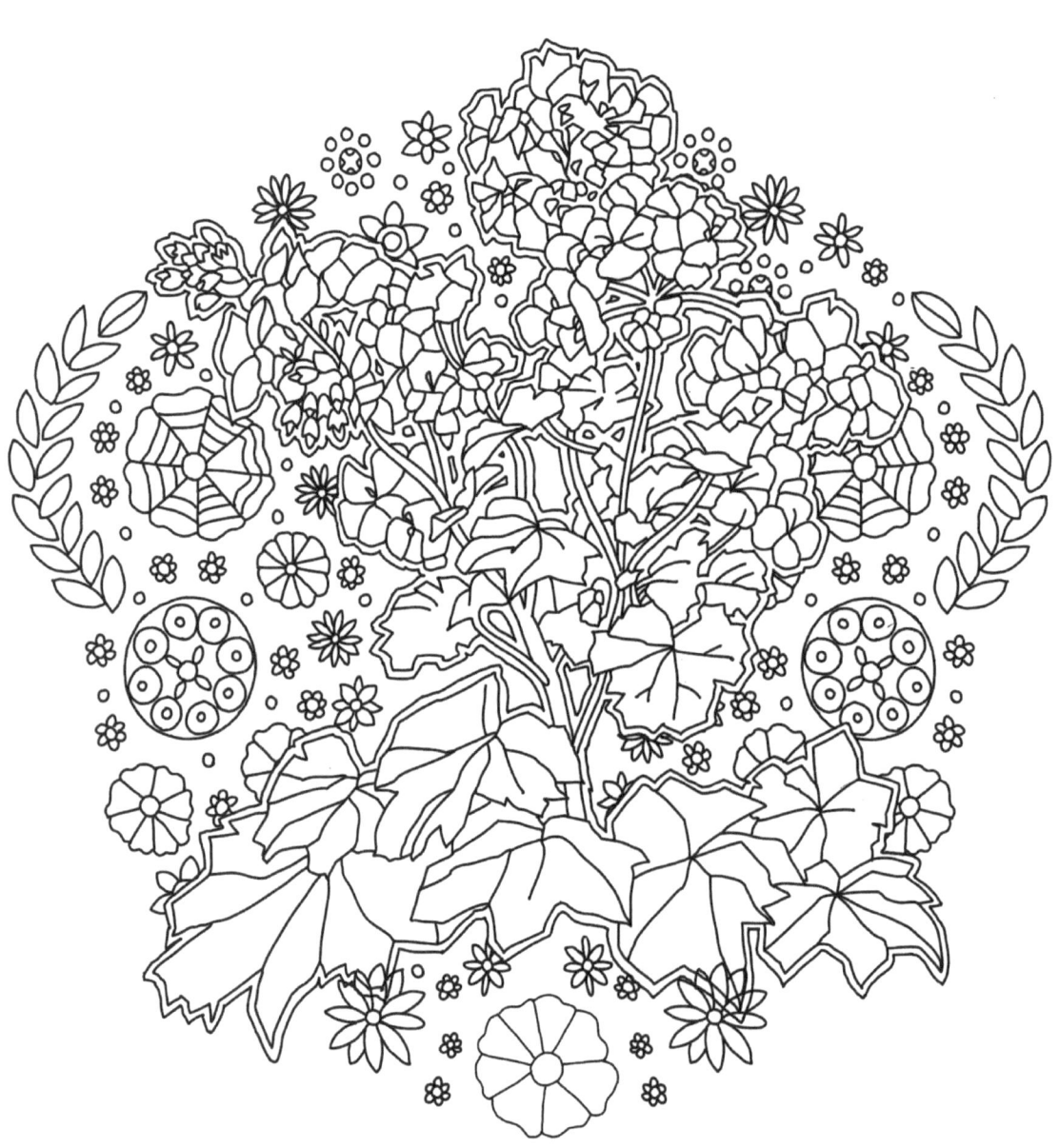

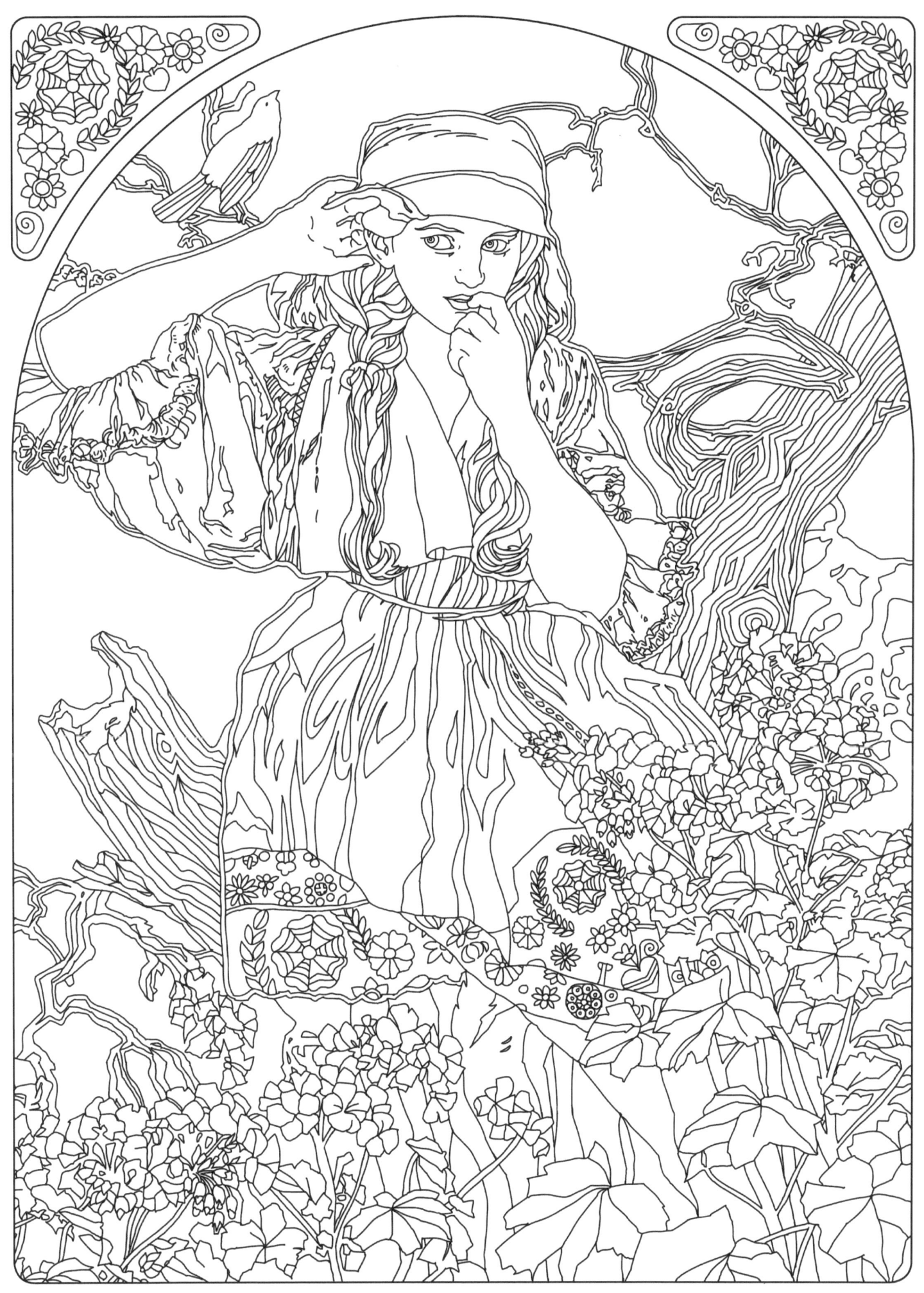

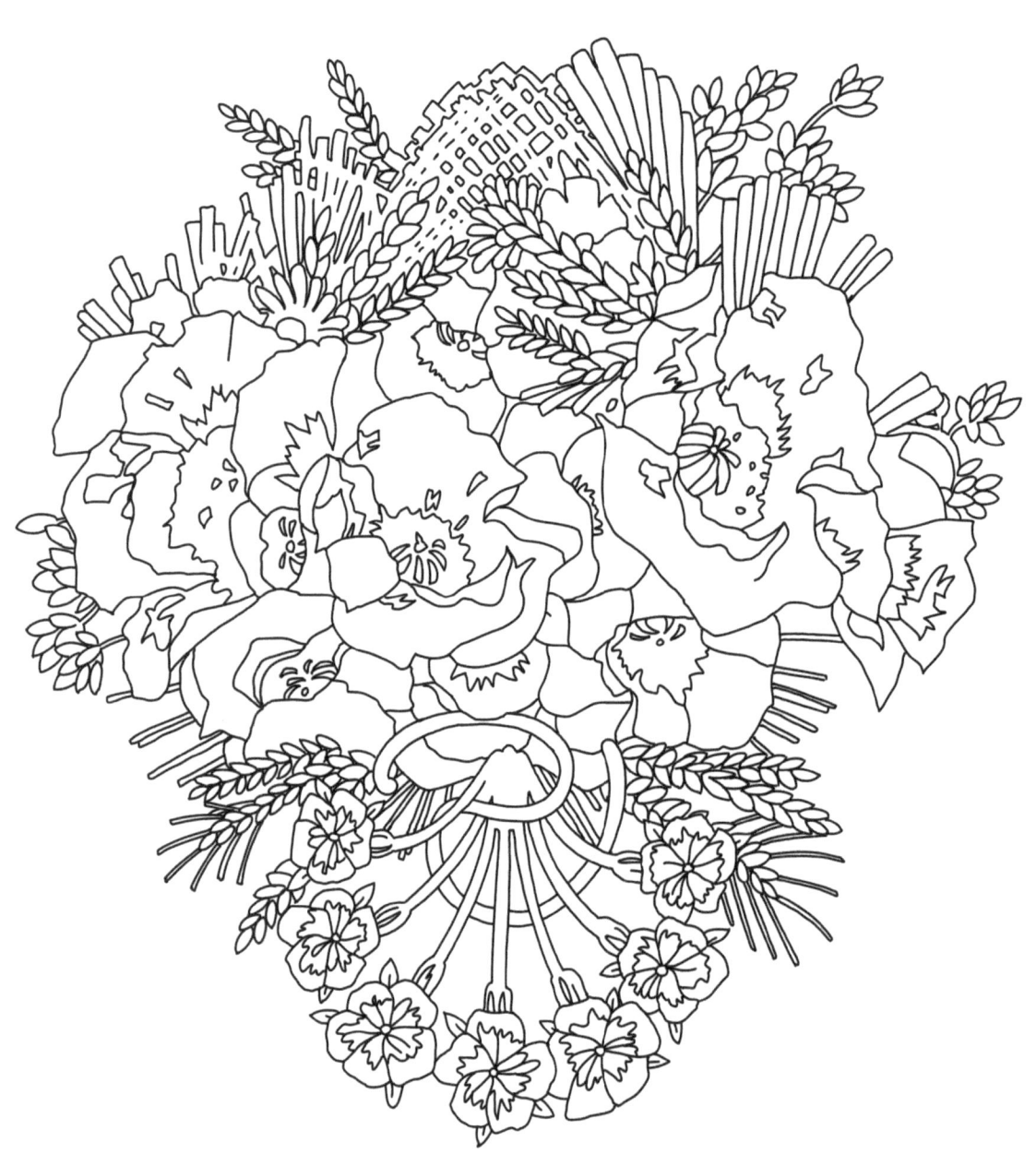

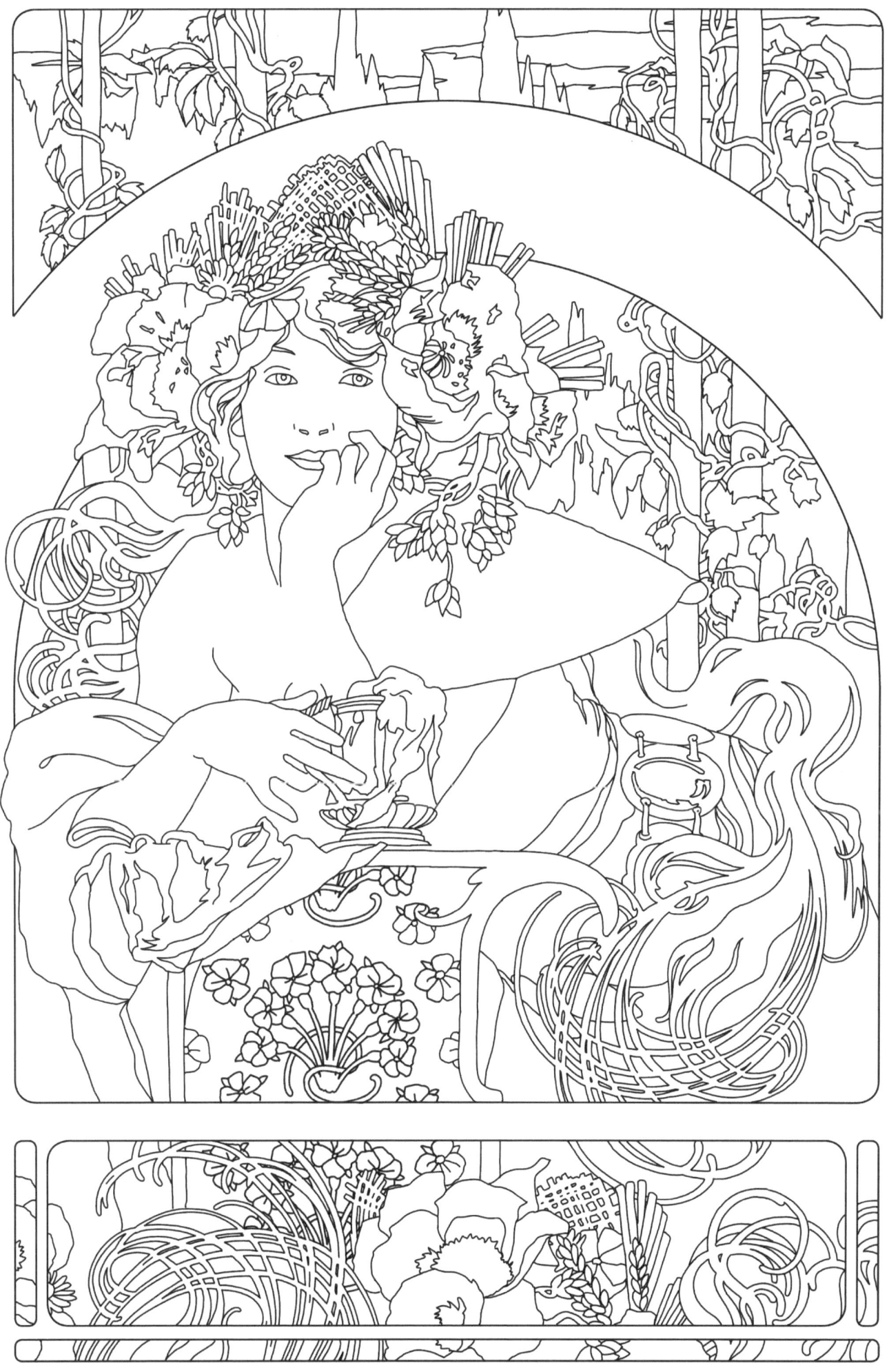

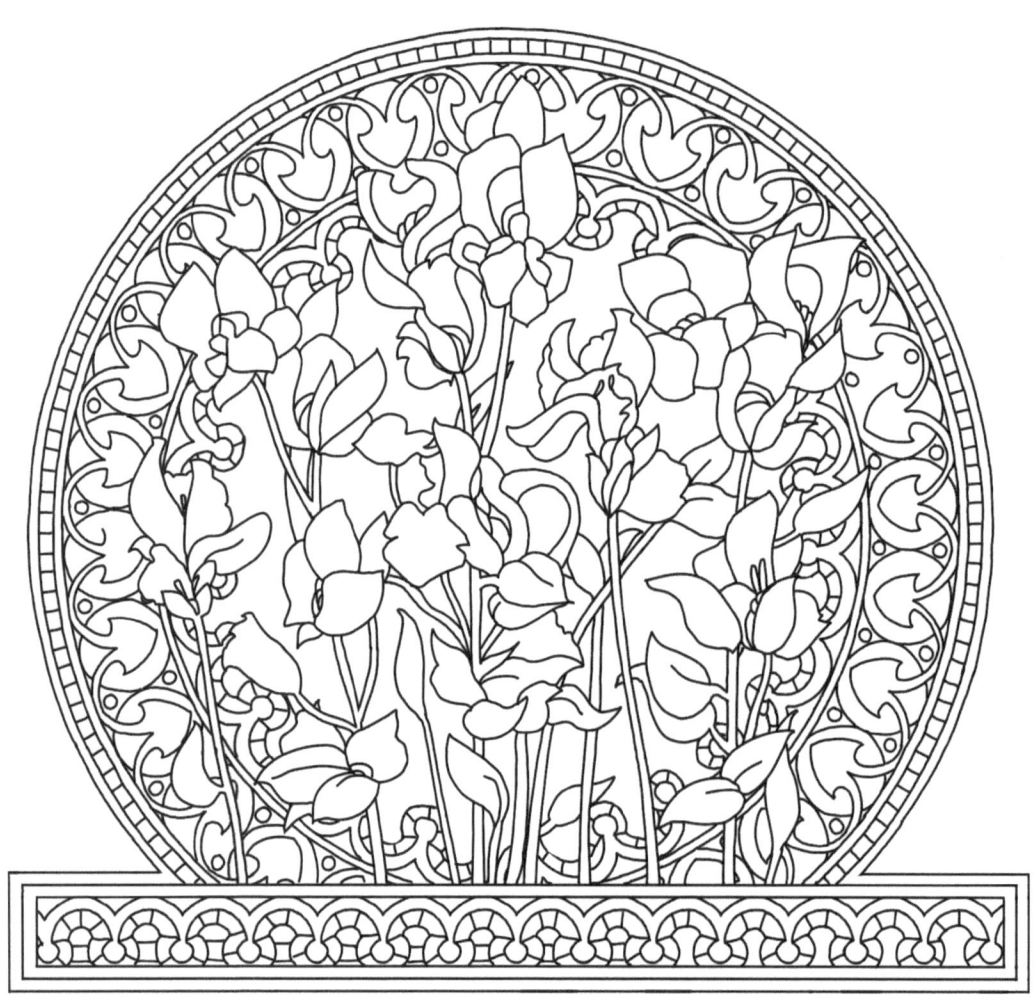

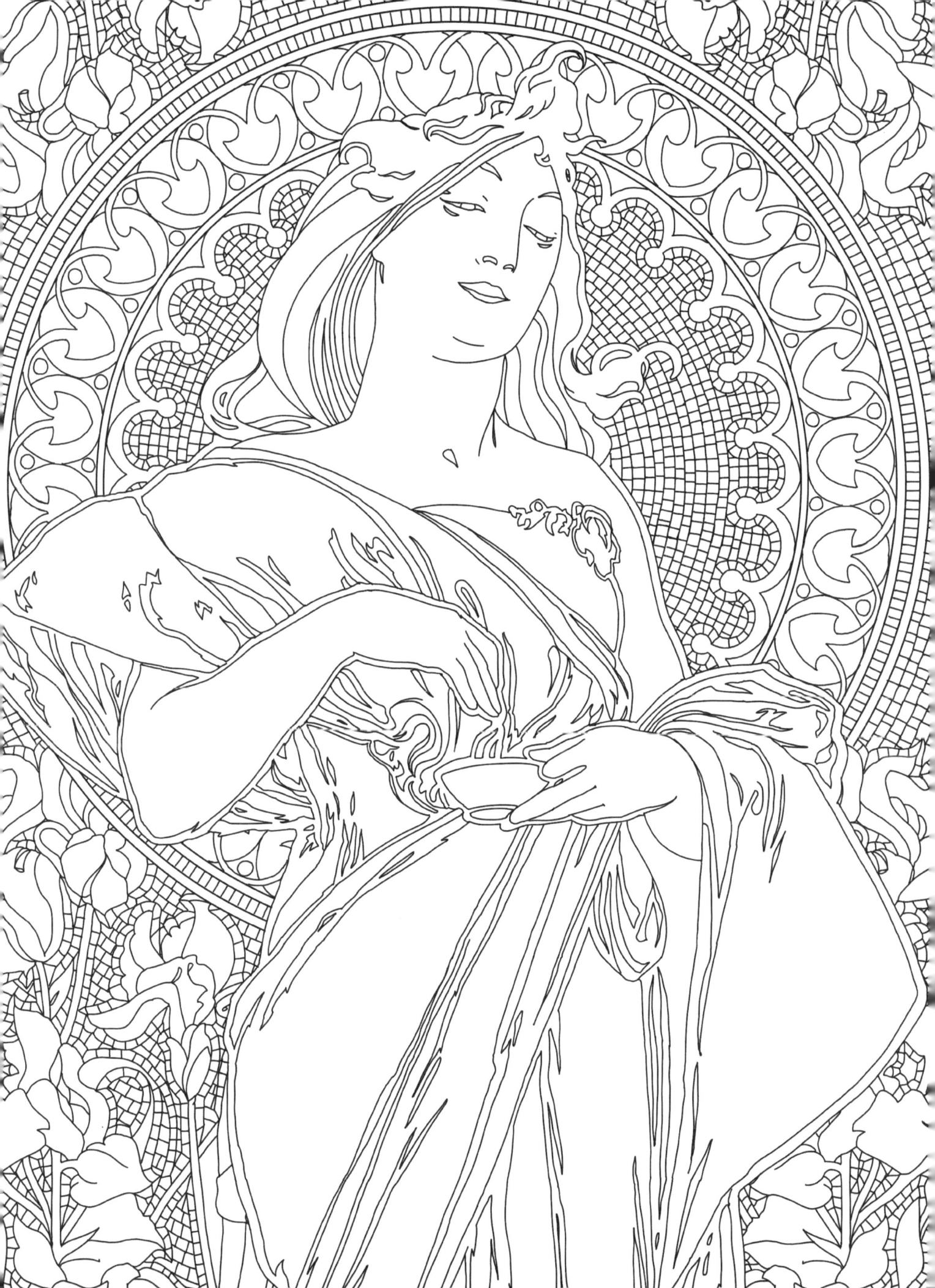